1

Henry Ford

Auto Tycoon

Henry Ford

Auto Tycoon

Insight and Analysis into the Man Behind the
American Auto Industry

JR MacGregor

Henry Ford – Auto Tycoon

Copyright © 2019 JR MacGregor

Published by CAC Publishing LLC

ISBN 978-1-950010-33-2 paperback

ISBN 978-1-950010-32-5 eBook

Contents

Introduction 8
Chapter 1 The Automobile 25
Chapter 2 Coming to America 42
Chapter 3 Henry Ford—An Overview 65
Chapter 4 Detroit 91
Chapter 5 The Ford Quadracycle 95
Chapter 6 ALAM & A Rising Star 102
Chapter 7 The Ford Motor Company 106
Chapter 8 Henry Ford and Thomas Alva Edison ... 110
Chapter 9 Ford and Edsel 126
Chapter 10 The Mind of a Genius 133
Conclusion 149

Introduction

Many men have been responsible for the rise of America—from Columbus to Lewis and Clark to today's titans of industry, including Bill Gates and Warren Buffet. Henry Ford stands atop this pantheon of titans for a number of reasons.

It is not because his wealth was greater than any of them. It is not. Rockefeller takes that title. It is also not because he invented a string of gizmos and machines. He didn't. That honor belongs to Edison. It is also not because he helped form the financial backbone of the United States. That title would easily go to J.P. Morgan.

Ford was none of these and often sorely misunderstood. He was cast with the devil for a few things he did in his life that may not be agreeable with the politics of today. He has been labeled a Nazi sympathizer. He was mentioned favorably in Hitler's *Mein Kampf* and awarded that country's highest honor that could be given to a foreigner—the Grand Cross of the German Eagle.

Ford purchased the *Dearborn Independent,* and in that paper, which had a circulation of almost one million, a series of articles were published that were anti-Semitic in nature. A lawsuitt was brought against him and the paper, but in sworn testimony many people familiar with the operation of the paper testified that Ford himself had no idea that the articles were published. It ended in a mistrial, and nothing more came of it, but the specter of anti-Semitism always lingered around him.

The series of articles that were printed in his paper were eventually collated into a book called *The International Jew.* For his views, Ford gained a friend in Hitler, and it cost him a great deal at home, but he wasn't an anti-Semite or a racist.

The problem with the anti-Semitic innuendos was accentuated by many smaller issues and Ford's failure to explain what actually happened and why he did it. What made it worse is that he was memorialized by Hitler. Just because he had opinions that were different from others didn't make him a monster, and just because Hitler wanted to implement his ideas in Germany doesn't make Ford the architect of Nazi Germany.

Mohandas Gandhi, the man who orchestrated India's independence, also drew the ire of the world for a short time when he was sympathetic to Hitler. Gandhi was willing to talk to him when others weren't. Gandhi even wrote to him. Those around Gandhi at the time were quick to jump on this act and condemn him.

By not seeing Ford or Gandhi as the kind of people they really were, you lose sight of what they contributed.

Ford and what he did for Americans and the world can't be thought of in terms of just automobiles. His goal was not just to make cars. It was to make inexpensive cars. Yes, other car manufacturers were also interested in making cheaper cars, but Ford was able to think from both an engineering and a humanitarian perspective. He didn't just want to put a car in every garage. He wanted to make sure that it was durable and lasted for a very long time.

The cars he manufactured that rolled off the assembly line every twenty-four seconds were workhorses and easily affordable. To be successful, Ford studied and devised ways to make parts in different ways and assemble them in ways that were not common at the time.

He also studied how human beings worked and thought they should be paid a living wage. He was the first person to think this way. Not even Carnegie or Rockefeller thought about treating workers the same way.

He insisted to his partners that his workers must be paid $5 per day. This may not seem like much today, but this was back in the early 1900s. A dollar in 1920 had the same purchasing power as $13 does today, which means that the average factory worker was taking home $65 per day. It was unheard of at the time. In fact, when Ford worked for the Edison Illuminating Company in Detroit as Chief Engineer, he made the same amount.

Ford thought people should be paid for the worth they brought to the table. He eventually raised those wages and even gave every employee a share of the company's profits. In return, he was rewarded with an endless supply of labor. Everyone wanted to work at the Ford plant.

He was, however, a strict employer and demanded a lot from his workers. They were rewarded handsomely not just in above-normal wages but also with better working conditions than could be found in most other factories. He wanted them to live in good conditions and be able to look after their families.

The amount of money he gave his workers earned him a reputation, and he demanded that everyone put in an honest day's work. They knew that if they did poorly they would be fired and that a hundred men were outside waiting for a job and could take their place.

Ford was indeed a genius and was always thinking ahead. Since he wanted a flawless and uninterrupted assembly line, he didn't want his workers worrying about what might be going on at home. Most of the time a man worries about money and looking after his family. To keep their minds on their work, he paid them well. He also didn't want them to be upset and go on strike to disrupt operations. He calculated that it was better to always pay the workers a good wage than to deal with disruptions.

To be able to pay above-market wages and produce high-quality products meant higher costs. Most manufacturers thought that the only way high costs could be balanced was by selling expensive cars, yet Ford was able to sell a large number of cars because he kept the price low and made money on the volume sold.

To be able to keep the assembly line constantly humming, he standardized the parts to such a high degree that you could move a line so quickly that a car would take about ninety minutes to go from the start of the line to the end of the line. In a day, he could make over a thousand cars due to his innovation of the moving assembly line.

The moving assembly line is not like what you would find in many car factories back then. In those days, cars were made by specialists, who would mill around the car doing different things. Each person would have many responsibilities, and days or weeks would be needed to complete just one car.

In a moving assembly line, the track that carries the unassembled vehicle would be constantly moving at a crawl. The worker would be installing something on it while walking along the car from a certain point on the line to the next point. He would then come back and get started on another car. The stations were timed carefully, and the workers would not have an opportunity to talk or be distracted. The job was so simple, though, that even a child could do it. Ford made sure to keep each job as simple as possible.

This was Ford's greatest contribution—the moving assembly line. He tied a rope to the front of the car (n tracks), and that motor would pull the car at a certain rate while the workers worked on it. Each event was timed so that the cars would take approximately the same length of time. The design of the car was integrated into the design of the assembly line. Parts were not made just for the car but also on how it would fare on the moving assembly line. If the part was too complex or required too much attention and a longer time to install, it was replaced with something that was easier. In Ford's way of doing things, he didn't just design the car. He also included the process of building it at the same time.

That is one reason why all Ford Model Ts were black in color. At that time, black paint was the fastest to dry and the easiest to apply. It allowed the assembly line to move faster.

He also didn't include any other colors because that would complicate the process and raise the price. He is quoted as saying, "People can have whatever color car they wanted as long as it was black."

He thought of everything right down to the last bolt, nut, and cotter pin. He thought about where each would go and in what order. Then he would stretch the sequence out on a line and test it, which would result in the shortest time on the assembly line.

At first, the Model T took twelve and a half hours to build. With further improvement, it took six hours and then just ninety-three minutes. The basic idea that Ford took as an example of this came from a meat-packing plant in Chicago. The butchers would hang the animal overhead and pass it along a line of workers who would skin, slaughter, process, and pack the meat from one station to the next.

In the same way, it wasn't just the car that was assembled that way. Many parts also needed assembly. For the car to be priced at less than $900, they had to get this process right.

Instead of having a magneto or a headlamp that involved many parts built by one person, Ford recognized that one person would work faster if they only had to do one task. So they broke up the assembly of even smaller parts. The magneto, for example, was broken up and had an assembly line of twenty-nine stations. Instead of just one man making one magneto, twenty-nine stations would come together to make the magneto as it passed from one man to the next. It stayed for only a few seconds at each station, and that took only five minutes to make each magneto. When they first started, it took one man more than thirty minutes to do it, and the reject rate was high. With twenty-nine men doing one part each and each of them being an expert at that part of it, the reject rate of the final assembly dropped drastically.

Such improvements and across the individual lines of assembly for all the parts allowed for $1,000 per car, which was his original threshold to drop the price to $350. The affordability goal was achieved, but Ford didn't stop there. He kept going until the Model T was able to come out of the plant every twenty-four seconds and the price of the vehicle had dropped below $300 each. It was 1927, and more than 15,000,000 Model Ts had been made, and one out of every two cars in America at the time was a Model T.

That price point altered the face of America. The terms *urban* and *suburban* were introduced into the vernacular from that point on because there was no longer any need for workers to live close to where they worked where it was congested and smoggy. They could now move out of the city and live somewhere that was better to raise their family and then drive to work in the morning. It is almost what we do today in larger cities, and that was created by the revolution that Henry Ford inspired.

Ford's objective resulted in improvements in so many areas. From the rapid assembly of the car and the lower costs to the quality of the car were unheard of at the time.

He looked at every detail, including hiring highly qualified machinists to make better quality parts so that they mated perfectly when assembled. They also made sure that the parts were easily accessible so that the owner could maintain it. It was a level of efficiency and effectiveness that was unheard of at the time.

This level to which Ford aspired in his endeavors is usually lost in the enigma of the story and the casual narrative that follows typical quotes and common anecdotes. But to find the genius of this man, one has to look at the lineage he came from—not just because we are slaves to our ancestors—but because Henry Ford was inspired by his family, including their hardships.

One of the things you can see from this was his friendship with the man who eventually solved the problem of the blithe potato that caused the Potato Famine in Ireland, which caused his family's sufferings and the reason they emigrated.

Many other clues point to Ford's sensitivity to his past. The home that Henry built in Dearborn was named Fairlane. When the Fords first moved to Cork from their farm, they lived on Fair Lane, the street where they sought shelter before leaving for Canada.

The life that Ford lived was influenced by William, his father, but it was done in opposition to what his father had envisioned for him. It would come to pass that whatever disappointed William about his son, Henry would feel the same way about his own son.

The disappointments were not about the failures of the subsequent generation but the decision by the next generation to not do things the way the older generation had prescribed.

William had wanted Henry to build up the farm, but Henry wanted to mechanize everything around him. Henry wanted his son, Edsel, to manage the plant with stricter hands, but Edsel wanted to do it with a gentler touch.

To each man, his son was a bit of a disappointment; to each son, his father was someone they could not live up to. What was common among all of them was that they were all stubborn.

Henry had troubles in his life that took him through periods of uncertainty. The investments he had solicited to build a company around his first vehicle didn't yield anything, and neither did the second.

He was almost forty years old and had not yet made a name for himself, but, more importantly, he had not accomplished what he had set out to do. The words of his father and the direction he had been given as a child kept playing in his head. "Maybe he should have stuck to farming." "Maybe he should have done what his father had wanted." An avalanche of thoughts plagued him, but Clara, his wife, always stood by his side.

It was Clara who pointed him in the right direction while they tried to make ends meet. It was because of her and Thomas Edison that he kept pursuing his dream. Thomas Edison was one of Ford's closest friends. The two of them would take annual vacations together, and President Harding and his team of Secret Service agents once went along.

The idea of studying about a man is to see his accomplishments as much as his mistakes. The best way to succeed in life is to look at the mistakes others have made and learn from them and also look at the achievements others have made and adapt them to your own life.

Reading about Ford should not be limited to mere inquisitiveness of places and dates, gossip and hearsay. It is about looking at him with the intent to understand yourself and your potential.

After all, we are all geniuses trying to make it in a world that others have already learned about and have already passed through. That is the important aspect of any biography, be it Carnegie, Rockefeller, Morgan, or even Mahatma Gandhi.

As we condense his life, it is important to understand where a man came from as much as it is to understand the reasons why he did what he did. It is also important to take as an example what he did and what he said and try to place these in the context of his vision. The best way is to look at things is as a student.

It is never beneficial for the student to look at things from a single point in time or space. Rather, it is important to look at the life of a man using the threads that link him to his past and the rails that connect him to the future.

A man's accomplishment is about many things, but most importantly it's about what he believes. Henry Ford believed in a world that was very different from the one he lived in. He believed in a world that was more efficient, and he was instrumental in bringing that about.

Take his production line. What is a moving assembly line if not a perfect picture of efficiency. That was the doing of Henry Ford. It is not as simple as one may think to come up with the results Ford did. It took vision to start, tenacity to overcome, patience to endure, and humility to learn. Ford was all these things and more. That was the essence of his actions.

But lest we misunderstand one simple and glaring truth, Ford was, like us, just human. He made his share of mistakes. He had his share of bias and prejudices and weaknesses. But that is what it means to be human. Everyone is similar in that regard. They do not know what they do, but the brief glimpse they do get and figure something out is when the rest of us need to look at it and learn from it for what it is. But if we make the mistake of judging the bad and forgetting the good, then we lose the opportunity to learn and become better.

Chapter 1 The Automobile

The last century and a half has been to automobiles what the Cambrian explosion had been to life on earth. From our grandparents' generation to ours today, the leap in technology, availability, prevalence, and diversity of automobiles has risen at an unfathomable rate and with unrelenting persistence. This has had a significant impact on the productivity and advancement of our lives but also has had some detrimental repercussions in terms of the environmental impact. Overall, however, the good has mostly outweighed the bad.

When humans first came out of Africa two million years ago and fanned across the globe, they did so on foot. They diffused across the globe organically like salt diffusing in unstirred water, eventually occupying almost every corner of the globe that was connected by land. That rate of diffusion was a function of a number of factors but was mostly limited to whether or not food was available or if predators were present, creating a hostile environment.

Humans were extremely adept bipeds, able to walk, jog, and sprint, which combined with our natural sense of curiosity was the core impetus to the spread of humanity across the planet.

We didn't just pick up and walk. We were even able to carry loads over long distances. What we were limited by was how much we could carry, which determined the supplies we needed and how far we could go. More food and water meant we could go longer before refills. It also determined how much shelter we could take with us, i.e., tents and tools.

Nonetheless, our ability to plan and carry what was needed on a trip combined with our curiosity to explore what was over the horizon gave us the impetus to explore. Exploration is in our genes.

It was a fairly unique ability in the animal kingdom—to be able to load ourselves with the burden and move long distances. Camels and horses, popular beasts of burden, didn't have the ability to load their backs and move great distances. Yet, they had the strength and structure to do it.

Left to their own devices, animals would just move, unencumbered, on their own, carrying their own weight. It wasn't until humans were able to domesticate them and load them with cargo that we were able to increase our cargo and extend our range. Walking had been our sole mode of mobility for two million years before we conscripted animals to do it for us. That evolution happened about six thousand years ago.

The point to note is acceleration. We walked for two million years; then we used beasts of burden for six thousand years; then we advanced to mechanized transportation. The time it took from one mode to the next went from two million years to just six thousand.

After six thousand years, we mechanized, and the first form of mechanized transportation was the locomotive. British engineer Richard Trevithick built the first steam locomotive in 1804, which revolutionized mass transportation of people along great distances.

That invention soon found its way to the New World, and in 1827, just twenty-three years later, the Baltimore-Ohio Railroad became the first railway line in the United States.

The transportation game can't be seen as one by itself. Just because you can build a bicycle or a tricycle is not going to have a significant impact on society in general. To be able to make a large enough difference, it has to be able to move a large number of people over great distances.

The train fulfilled that need, and although caravans of horse-drawn carriages transported frontiersman across the harsh unpopulated lands, it was the railroad that led to wide areas of the country being populated. Without trains, cities could not have been a reality.

That was the second land transportation revolution, with the taming of animals as beasts of burden being the first.

If the train gave the power of exodus to the masses, what came next was an even more powerful iteration in the transportation saga. It was the automobile and its ability to move individuals anywhere without the necessary infrastructure of rails that characterized rail travel. The difference was that this new form of transportation allowed individuals to travel where they wished in a direct manner.

The automobile had two aspects that needed to come together: (1) an engine to drive it and (2) a structure to be able to carry the payload and the power plant. The problem was not the carriage. Any horse carriage could be adopted for the purpose, or so they thought. The real problem was to create an engine that had enough torque to propel the carriage forward.

A few men were trying to perfect the formula. Two in particular were highly successful—Karl Friedrich Benz and Gottlieb Wilhelm Daimler. They were working independently just sixty miles apart and came up with the necessary elements for a working vehicle.

Benz not only managed to design an effective contraption that acted as a four-wheeled carriage, but he also invented a successful two-stroke engine to propel the carriage. Daimler, also an engineer, developed the liquid petroleum four-stroke engine and had a carriage built to accommodate it.

Benz and Daimler had different philosophies in mating car to the engine and so had fairly distinct outcomes.

Cars at that time were not envisioned to travel over asphalt but just on dirt roads. That meant there was no need for massive construction costs, such as was involved with railroads, which required sovereign bonds to be issued in the early nineteenth century.

Paved roads were good but not necessary. These cars that were at the genesis of the age of the personal automobile still did not represent a transportation revolution. These new cars were crude, expensive to build, not affordable by most people, and still pretty much a novelty.

The potential for such an invention, however, was not lost on the strategic thinkers of the era. Most could see that the power of mechanized personal transport would be revolutionary, especially since it didn't need to have rails, a specialist engineer to drive it, or an animal to pull it. Anyone could drive an automobile and take it anywhere.

For the automobile to be widely accepted, it had to be rapidly built, affordable, easily powered, and easily driven. At the time Benz and Daimler made the first gasoline vehicles, just the opposite was true. They were slow to build because each unit was handbuilt, taking more than a month to build just one vehicle. That made the whole process expensive, and what was worse was that the materials needed for them came from still burgeoning industries.

The internal combustion engine had not been perfected, generating only about half horsepower and topping out at about 750 rpm. Fuel sources were still uncertain, labor was mostly uneducated, and rubber for tires was not prevalent. The driving issue in all this was economies of scale. None of the sub-industries had it.

Another problem in the development of the automobile also slowed its advance. To be affordable to the masses, a number of technological advancements needed to be made. From metallurgy to engineering to even the choice of propellant, numerous areas had yet to come together to make the automobile viable.

Without sufficient development, the necessary technology was lacking, and the cost was expensive. With expensive cars, only a few could afford them, which meant there wasn't enough money to direct toward investment and development. It also meant insufficient volume to demand development of other areas, such as fuel, tires, and upholstery. The ripple effect upstream in the nonexistent industry was having a hard time taking hold.

The third transportation revolution was sputtering to life but was not quite there yet. To be considered a transportation revolution, it had to alter the landscape in a profound and widespread manner in the way trains did before it and domesticated animals. But it didn't stop there.

In the United States, another problem needed to be overcome. It was of a legal nature and one that stifled the nascent growth of automobile innovation. An American patent attorney by the name of George Baldwin Selden was quick to realize that Benz's and Daimler's inventions would be a major factor in the development of transportation around the world, and he wanted to profit from that in the United States.

He was what many called the original "patent troll." Patents were designed to protect real inventors and their intellectual property, but Selden decided to sketch out his ideas similar to the cars that Benz and Daimler had developed and filed that as his patent in the United States.

Since he was a patent attorney, he knew the tricks and strategies of U.S. patent law, and the loophole he exploited was how patents are granted in pending status.

The point of that patent strategy was to exploit the limited life of the patent from the day the patent is granted in full. Selden wanted to circumvent that because he didn't know when the automobile would become popular in the United States. He would update the patent every few months, which would return the patent to pending status. He finally filed the final patent in 1895, and that expired in 1912. It was U.S. Patent No. US549460A.

In it he deliberately mentioned that his idea to build this petroleum-powered vehicle was to increase the efficiency of a vehicle that would otherwise have to work on steam, which needs the vehicle to carry water to convert to steam and coal to heat water.

His business strategy worked. When the news of automobiles reached the United States, budding entrepreneurs and inventors leaped at the prospect of building the first American car.

The Electric Vehicle Co. decided in 1899 that they wanted to get into the gasoline-powered market and purchased the Selden patent for $5,000 and $5 per car in royalties. In today's dollars, that works out to be about a quarter of a million dollars plus royalties.

The Electric Vehicle Company, through their lawyers, started sending out cease and desist letters to manufacturers and warning them that they were infringing on the Selden patent. Many of the manufacturers completely disregarded the letter and went on with their business.

EVC eventually started filing suits against many of those carmakers. The manufacturer that was highest on their list to go after was the Winton Motor Carriage Company, owned by the Alexander Winton.

Winton was the fastest race car driver in America at the time, and his company had the largest share of the U.S. automobile market. It seemed best to sue him and claim back pay for all the cars he had sold up to that point. For Selden, this was always about the money.

Winton fought the Electric Vehicle Company for two years until 1902, when he began to think of a way to end the feud. Because of the problem between Winton and the Electric Vehicle

Company, several other automobile manufacturers united to form the Manufacturer's Mutual Association or the MMA.

It was founded by Frederic L. Smith and Henry Bourne Joy—Henry Bourne Joy was of the Packard Motor Car Company, and Frederic L. Smith was of the Olds Motor Works—a cofounder in fact—which created the Curved Dash Oldsmobile, the car that is credited as being the first to have been mass produced but was still very expensive.

Together, Joy and Smith said they wanted the royalties to be decreased and also wanted to take control of the licensing. In the end, the MMA was able to get control of the patent and the licensing in 1903.

It was also in 1903 that the organization was rechristened the Association of Licensed Automobile Manufacturers or ALAM. From there it evolved. The Electric Vehicle Company in concert with ALAM charged anyone who wanted to manufacture automobiles an annual fee of $5,000 and $15 per car as royalty. The proceeds were shared by ALAM, Electric Vehicle Company, and Selden.

ALAM's expressly stated purpose was to prevent anyone who seemed that they didn't know what they were doing and fly-by-night operators from setting up an automobile plant.

There were significant consequences to this move. First, it created a monopoly on the system. In addition to the licensing fee, not everyone who wanted to jump into the market was allowed to. There was no free enterprise in the industry, and the innovation that is needed in new industries was stifled by this unnatural requirement.

Second was that their patent was entirely undeserving. In many cases, it was a patent that had been obtained by the amalgamation of other ideas and used an engine that was wholly unsuitable for the task. In later years, it was found that if an engineer were to build a vehicle according to the plans that were submitted to the U.S. Patent Office, the resulting vehicle would not work very well.

The automobile has been a key factor in the development and advancement of human civilizations and societies. It is unique in its ability to provide mass transportation at an individual level. That is the true genius of cars. They represent the last-mile solution to mobility for a large number of people. Planes get you across continents, trains get you across long distances, but cars, in addition to being able to drive across regions, can also take you to and from major hubs to individual areas without the restriction of schedules.

Automobiles are the best of both worlds. Compared with the locomotive that provided mass mobility with little freedom to the passengers, automobiles provide mass mobility to individuals and the freedom to experience that mobility in any way they want.

The original car manufacturers in the United States, in the wake of Benz's and Daimler's invention in Germany, were focused on expensive vehicles that were handmade, inefficient, and had heavy engines.

concentrating on individuality rather than mass appeal.

Henry Ford did not invent the car. He did not invent the manufacturing process, and he did not build the engine. What he did was solve the last-mile problem of putting a car in every driveway by refining the production and design technology that allowed a car to be affordable for almost everyone.

It didn't matter if you built a car, for if you made it unaffordable, it would not solve the last-mile problem since most individuals would not be able to afford it. Ford was instrumental in doing that. He didn't ask for subsidies in making the car. He altered the design, the cost structure, and the manufacturing practices within the design and building elements. In other words, he built the car from the ground up, keeping in mind that it had to be cheap enough so that everyone could own one. That is what changed everything. His pioneering work was so effective that the typical one-car household became a two-car household within fifty years of Ford's Model T.

It wasn't just the automobile. It was the automobile for everyone, which meant that city planning could change. It was no longer necessary that homes be close to factories or offices. Communities could develop in the suburbs and alter the average way of life.

These effects and more were a direct consequence of Henry Ford.

Chapter 2 Coming to America

In 1832, Samuel and George Ford arrived in Michigan Territory to stake their claim on frontier land. They left their father, William, and mother, Rebecca, as well as their elder brother, John, on the land the family was living on in Ireland.

At that time, Ireland was in economic flux, transitioning from military and shipping activities in the wake of the Napoleonic Wars to agriculture and transatlantic shipping.

The family that Samuel and George left behind continued to farm in Ballinascarty, a small farming community approximately twenty miles southwest of Cork.

Farmers here were used to a simple life, which was organized under a simple structure.

Landowners would rent out tracts of land to families, who would farm the land. As long as a family paid its rent, their livelihood was secure. Irish law back then prohibited landowners from evicting farmers as long as they paid the rent. It could even pass from one farmer to the next if he so assigned it, and the landowner would have to abide by the transition.

William Ford Sr. continued such a rental agreement with Jonas Starvell for twenty-three acres of farmland that their family had been on for some time. The house the Fords originally built remained for some time and passed to the farmers that took over after the Fords left.

Remnants of the stone cottage that William and Rebecca Jennings Ford (Henry Ford's great-grandparents) first built on Starvell's land still remain. The Irish countryside was peppered with other Ford family members renting land from other landowners. They are still there to this day.

Ireland's population was about eight million people at the turn of the century, and 40 percent of them depended exclusively on potatoes for sustenance. As such, farming in Ireland was focused primarily on potatoes. Dairy and berries were important as well but to a lesser degree.

Unlike today's dinner table with a variety of nutritional sources, from meats to salads and carbohydrates, Ireland in the 1800s was predominantly a one-staple economy. Meat was too expensive for most of the population and reserved for special occasions.

This potato-based menu was across the board. Whether you farmed the land or worked in a factory, almost everyone had one nutritional source for breakfast, lunch, and dinner. It was always potatoes. From potato soup to mashed potatoes to boxty, coddle, and colcannon, that's what was available.

The Ford family—brothers, sisters, cousins—were all diligent workers, which paid off in a stable farming life. They settled in one generation after the other on this farm.

Cork, the closest major city, survived becuse it was a port serving transatlantic trade. Of the three major cities of Dublin, Limerick, and Cork in this predominantly agricultural country, Cork was the smallest. That would eventually change when the Ford Motor Company set up a plant here in 1912.

John Ford, Henry Ford's grandfather, lived in the same stone cottage his father had on Starvell's property and continued the same farming practice his father did. An intervening event, however, caused John and his wife, Thomasina, to rethink their lives. In the Ford household was John, his wife, children, and his widowed mother. John's father, William, had passed some time earlier.

Potato Famine

The Potato Famine of 1849–1856 shook the lives of the Fords and almost every person in Ireland when a type of water mold spread across the potato farms in Ireland, causing an infection called the potato blithe. That event hit Ireland hard in many ways. Aside from affecting the potato crop thereby reducing the income of the farmer to zero, it directly altered the nutritional profile of part of the country, which had a knock-on effect across other agrarian and nonagrarian industries. The result was a widespread famine that created a financial catastrophe for the farmers who relied on the income from potatoes to pay the rent.

When the crops failed, the population subsequently descended into starvation and poor health. The five-year catastrophe caused more than one million deaths and spurred countless numbers of people to cross the Atlantic on less-than-safe contraptions that passed for ships.

The mortality rate on board these ships, called Coffin Ships, was extraordinarily high, as many people were ridden with typhus and infected with lice. The lice compounded the problem with the typhus, as it was the vector that transmitted the pathogen. Even a healthy person who boarded any of these Coffin Ships at Cork had a very high chance of falling ill out on the Atlantic, as the inexperienced crew took anywhere from three to six months to make the trip.

Out of the total farming population, more than five hundred thousand farmers were evicted over the five-year period. Out of that number, about 20 percent tried their luck by boarding these Coffin Ships. One hundred thousand Irishmen set sail, most of them already facing severe malnutrition and disease. The conditions on the ships exaggerated the malady, and one in five died on their way to British North America.

As for the Ford family, the loss of the crop due to the blithe epidemic that destroyed the potatoes caused them to lose their sole source of income. Without that income and without the prospect of being able to plant any more potatoes or buy seeds to plant other crops, they were not able to pay rent on the land. They were left with no choice and had to give up the land before they were evicted or jailed.

There was a grizzly aspect to this that affected the Fords and many in the same predicament. The agricultural industry around the mid-nineteenth century was dominated by landowners who were rather ruthless in their dealings with the farmers who rented their land. There were two kinds of these landowners in Ireland. One group would place the head of the delinquent household under arrest and kick the family out onto the streets without any prospect of shelter or food. That was the reality for many of the farmers.

The other option was that the farmers gave up the land and left whatever they built or had on the land, and the landowner would take possession of the land and rent it to someone else. The Fords were fortunate enough to have been able to do the latter.

With this little bit of luck in the midst of death and chaos around them, John Ford and Thomasina packed up what little else they had and walked the twenty miles to Cork in hope of better prospects. In tow were John's mother and his seven children, his brother Robert, and the Roberts family.

They stayed with relatives in a rented a house on Fair Lane in Cork and settled into 'the community along with little William (Henry Ford's father). They had little money but faced overwhelming hardships from food shortages and lack of resources. The poverty they faced was not individual. It was systemic.

Henry had heard stories from his father about the time the Fords were in Cork and where little William would go from house to house and sell eggs that he bought from one of the shops close by. Everyone in the neighborhood knew the Fords back then, as they were amiable and hospitable farmers who had been hit by the famine and came to the city. They made a living here as best they could, but with current conditions dire and future prospects dim, they had to make a hard decision on what to do next. A farmer without a farm is like a baker without an oven or a carpenter without tools. There would be no means to put food on the table and a roof overhead.

It is easy to discount the decision-making process in light of what we see around us in the U.S. today. There is a sense that the pull factor toward materialism, consumerism, quality, and standards of living are all excuses that a person might first face in their country of origin. Today, it may seem that immigration is fueled by something other than dire necessity (some are, but most aren't), but back then no one could deny that leaving the Old World and going to vast open spaces in the New World was a life or death decision that needed to be made. It's like being on the top floor of a burning skyscraper. Victims are even willing to take their chances when they jump out the window rather than be engulfed by the flames. The reasons for the Fords' inclination to travel were more about the push than about the pull.

Indeed, for the Fords and many others, going to America was a hard decision to make. It was not going to be a life spent on a bed of roses. No one who made their way to America in the mid-nineteenth century had delusions about that, but they did know that life in the unknown was better than the life facing certain death.

With a million people out of three million dead, the mortality rate gave potato-dependent Irishmen a 1-in-3 chance of survival. That may seem good odds when seen through the eyes of history, but when you have a family of nine—two parents and seven children—that means that three of your family members would not make it. Those are horrible odds, and those three are members of your own family. It's always harder when it's kin.

John and Thomasina thought long and hard while they made their living in a city that was on its downward swing. With the Napoleonic Wars over and the port business going through changes and relying on trade rather than military-related activities, everyone was going through adjustments.

Because it was a time when nutrition was minimal, it meant falling ill frequently—more so for the parents than for the children and more so for the mother than the father. Thomasina sacrificed much of what she had so that her children could have the first pick at the meager meals and her husband could have what he needed to expend on labor. In time, Thomasina was perpetually ill due to what must have been an extremely low immune system.

Not only did they have to stretch the food, but they also knew that they had to save as much as they could to be able to get passage on one of the many Coffin Ships that were sailing to the New World.

Conditions on the Coffin Ships were more than what most of us today can imagine. They were crowded with improper and unhygienic facilities. Families who were ill and destitute were making a last-ditch effort aboard poorly built vessels that were built to accommodate the masses trying to flee Ireland.

There were two points of destination that they could choose from. They could sail to either New York or Quebec, the latter being significantly cheaper than the former. As such, the usual choice was to head for Quebec and then make the trek down to the United States by land.

The Fords saved all they could, led simple lives, and decided to cast their lot to the winds across the Atlantic. They sold what little they had, packed up the family, and headed for Quebec. Along with John, Thomasina, and the children, his mother, and brother Robert (and his wife and children) tagged along. If it weren't for the famine, the Fords would not have left Ireland.

The trip was approximately three thousand miles from Cork Harbor to the St. Lawrence River in Quebec, which is almost the same distance as the crow flies from New York to San Francisco.

The journey would normally take five weeks on a normal ship but took longer on a Coffin Ship. The ships' owners were not expecting many of the passengers to survive the trip and were in it to make money without providing proper food, water, and berths. Many of those on these ships were buried at sea. The captain and crew were not well trained and barely satisfied the minimum to get the boat across the Atlantic. They ships were also well insured and worth more sunk than if they made the trip.

One in five of the one hundred thousand who set sail perished at sea or at the medical inspection station. Thomasina was one of those people who didn't make it. She was buried at sea.

William was in his early twenties at this time and took it very hard as did the rest of the family. As painful as it was, however, it was also fortunate that the loss the family faced was limited to just one person. After getting to North America and settling down, John never remarried.

As a family that had survived the famine intact and being almost home free, for Thomasina to pass away at the last turn had a chilling effect on them. Out of the eighty thousand Irish who did make it alive, half of them remained in Quebec and traveled inland. The other half crossed the border into the territories or into the northern part of the United States.

Upon arriving at the Saint Lawrence River, the Fords entered the medical inspection facility before being allowed to enter Canada legally. It is worth noting that Canada was under the British Empire at the time and thus did not have the same immigration issues of entry as those arriving at New York's Ellis Island.

Once they arrived in Quebec, the Ford family— John, his children, and John's mother made their trek across the U.S. border by foot. Robert Ford and his family remained in Canada.

John Ford

John Ford was Henry Ford's grandfather. He led the family from Ballinascarty to Cork and then across the Atlantic. In his care were three

Detroit is located in Wayne County.

generations of Fords. They crossed the border from Quebec into the United States on their way to Michigan. They headed here because John's two brothers, Samuel and George, who had left Ireland almost a decade earlier, had settled in Wayne County, Michigan. Thomasine's family, the Smiths, was also in Wayne County at the time.

Once arriving in Dearborn, they lived with Samuel Ford's family and immediately thought about buying his farm. The idea of owning a farm was something that was revered and cherished. The Irish had lived for generations in a land tenancy structure where they farmed the land they did not own. The landowners were revered and respected no matter how brutal some of them could be. That same respect had created a desire in the hearts and minds of the Fords who came to Michigan.

John Ford wanted to become a landowner and work his own soil. Once they settled down on Samuel's farm and helped him with the chores, John and William set about to buy their own land.

They worked as much as they could to raise the money doing manual labor in the surrounding area and on the rail that was being constructed between there and Detroit, about seven miles away.

They eventually found a close Irish friend of theirs, Henry Maybury, living in Redmond Township near Detroit. He was willing to sell John eighty acres of virgin forest land in Redmond. The total price was $350, but John and William had only $200.

They paid that $200 to Maybury in 1848 and owed the rest. William, a skilled carpenter in Ireland, continued to put his carpentry to work on the railroad, and both John and William set out to pay off the remaining $150. One of the carpentry jobs he took on was for Patrick O'Hearn. Patrick had a large establishment, which was one of the larger employers in the neighborhood. Patrick and his wife didn't have children of their own and had adopted an orphan by the name of Mary Litogot.

By December 1850, William had helped his father settle the mortgage, and John finally became a landowner.

William Ford

William Ford was born in 1826 in the cottage where his father and mother lived. He trained as a carpenter while working on the farm in Cork and was handy in many ways.

He grew up to be a slender young man with the trademark Ford frame and high cheekbones.

To say he was a dyed-in-the-wool farmer would not be far from the truth, but to think he had much interest in farming would not be accurate. He saw farming as a necessity and carpentry as a means to advance. Either way, William was very strong willed and used to harsh conditions and was always willing to work hard.

He was also a very conventional and thoughtful young man. He was creative in his own way and very interested in advancing the farm in nontraditional ways, such as thinking how to mechanize operations on the farms where he worked with his father.

William was ambitious. He continuously sought ways to improve the farm, and his efforts paid off. The farm did well, and both John and William grew more prosperous as the years unfolded.

He still continued to build houses and made a name for himself as an able carpenter. His friendship with the O'Hearns after he helped build their house was also a positive factor in his life. Patrick O'Hearn was a powerful ally to have and a person who would easily recommend or assist William whenever needed.

William also remained friends with the Maybury family. The Marburys went on to become one of the most influential and wealthy Irish immigrants in the Detroit-Dearborn area.

At the time when William was helping the O'Hearns build their home, he met Mary Litogot, the adopted daughter of the family. Mary was born in Michigan and just eleven years old when William was working on the O'Hearn family home.

Her natural parents who had emigrated from Belgium passed away when Mary was still a young child and left her to be adopted by an Irish family when she was three years old. The O'Hearns were well-to-do and had enrolled Mary in private school. There she was raised with proper etiquette and science, which resulted in a young lady who was intelligent and witty. They also raised her with many Irish practices and culture.

William continued to do whatever jobs that came his way, especially since Detroit was starting to transition from being frontier land to something more established, especially along the waterfront.

In 1858, William had saved enough to buy forty acres of his father's farm for $600 and closed the transaction on September 15. John sold the southern half of the property to William and the northern half of the property to William's young brother, Samuel, for the same price.

As he was climbing the rungs of opportunity, William fell in love with Mary Litogot. They had been friends since meeting when he was working on the O'Hearn house, and then they dated for almost a decade.

They were married in April 1861, eleven years after first meeting. The wedding was held at the home of Thomas Maybury in Detroit. While this was happening in the relative peace of the Michigan landscape, the first shell had exploded in the air above Fort Sumter in South Carolina. It heralded the arrival of one of the deadliest times in American history, but all that seemed a world away to the newlyweds.

She conceived during the first year after the wedding and gave birth the following year, but the child died soon after birth. Mary, who was naturally kind and loving, was devastated. It was something that was common in those days of frontier living, but it was still a painful experience.

Once married, William left his father's farm in Redmond and moved into the cottage that he had originally helped Patrick O'Hearn build. When they moved in, William decided to design and build a much larger home so that the two families would have plenty of room, and they also knew that more children would soon be on the way.

He ended up building a seven-room mansion for both families to live in. William and Mary stayed here for the rest of their lives and eventually inherited the house William built and 90 acres of land that belonged to Patrick O'Hearn. They renamed the place Greenfield Village.

While the war may have been a long way off, it was still, nonetheless, a major part of everyone's life and concern in the little town of Dearborn, Michigan. The Dearborn Arsenal, built in 1830, was one of the few locations where the U.S. government stored weapons and ammunition. Soldiers on their way to battle would stop at this armory to purchase and pick up weapons. It was a pretty busy place during the Civil War.

Dearborn Arsenal was just about a mile west of Greenfield Village.

Since William remained a British subject in the United States after his arrival and until 1864, he was not conscripted or bound to join the military during the Civil War. This allowed him to focus on his business and build the two farms, while most other Michigan male residents were drafted to serve the war effort.

With his father's guidance and his wife's support, he soon developed their family farm to be one of the most successful in the area. His brother's farm in the north was also doing well. The other successful farm in the area belonged to his cousin, William Samuel Ford—the farm where they had lived when they first arrived in Michigan.

By the end of 1862, Mary was expecting again. The Fords had comfortably taken up residence at the O'Hearn's, and the new mansion was ready. Mary gave birth to their second child, Henry Ford, on July 30, 1863.

Earlier that same month the Civil War had turned the corner. What was certain doom for the Union just prior to July that year during the Battle of Gettysburg changed course in Lincoln's favor.

William Ford had always adopted a forward-thinking mannerism in everything he was involved in. Whether it was designing and building a mansion or the way he managed the farms he was in charge of or owned, he was always innovating. He soon became well respected in the Dearborn area and also became deacon of the church and was elected to the school board and justice of the peace.

Chapter 3 Henry Ford—An Overview

At the time of Ford's birth, gasoline-powered automobiles were nonexistent. Karl Benz, the man who invented the automobile and the engine that powered it, was just nineteen years old and still at the University of Karlsruhe on his way to becoming a mechanical engineer.

America, which was a house still divided by war, experienced divided rates of prosperity. The North did better than before the war, while the South did considerably worse since most of the battles took place in the South and, consequently, suffered more destruction.

That meant two things: (1) farmers in the North had more opportunities since they did not have to rebuild, and (2) farmers and the industrial infrastructure were already owner operated and not overly dependent on slave labor.

The South's infrastructure was destroyed, and it had to restrict and restructure the way it mobilized its labor force. This created a net flow of benefit from commerce to the North, which set up foundations for prosperity. Farmers in the South, however, were entrenched in labor practices, even if they believed that all men were created equal.

What was actually a boon to farming became its bane in the wake of the Emancipation Proclamation of 1863. With that order, more than 3.5 million slaves, or absolutely every slave that was brought into the country or born here, was given freedom, which altered the course of businesses in the South and, more importantly, their cost structure. Putting aside the moral issues of slavery, whichever side of the debate one may be on, what happened in 1863, the year that Henry Ford was born, was significant in the way he redesigned the labor force and utilization of work to propel the Second Industrial Revolution.

At the same time, the United States was actively opening its doors to immigration. Between 30,000 and 450,000 immigrants were arriving annually from Europe and the rest of the world, and this created a very large supply of labor in the country. While Ford's River Rouge plant was being built, immigration had risen to between 600,000 and 1.2 million per year, creating an even greater supply of labor.

Putting aside his sympathies and advocacy of Nazi Germany and accusations of anti-Semitism, Ford was not a racist. In fact, it was impossible for him to see anything else besides a fellow human being when someone stood in front of him. He didn't see color, height, weight, or religion. He did, however, recognize intelligence.

The River Rouge plant was the largest integrated manufacturing facility the world had ever seen. It employed more than one hundred thousand people who were housed in more than ninety buildings. These contained everything from convenience stores to offices, steel mills to machine shops, assembly lines to stores, and even fire departments and hospitals.

To staff this facility, he relied on the abundant supply of labor, both local and immigrant. He even set up schools to teach immigrants English, and when they graduated, he would have ceremonies to welcome them into the Ford family and to the larger family as Americans.

Henry Ford was a very compassionate person, but he was biased and had his quirks, one being that he considered a person's intelligence and ability to learn as their most important trait.

He was generous in the way he paid his workers in the factories; in fact, he paid the highest rates for a day's labor at the Ford Motor Company factory. When the average annual salary in the United States was $450, Ford started his factory workers off at $5 per day, or $25 per week, or $1,200 per year—significantly higher than the national average at the time.

These people were factory line workers who didn't need or have tertiary education or actually any education at all. Many of them didn't even speak English because they were new immigrants.

intelligence, integrity, and self-respect.

In return, he insisted that they display intelligence, integrity, and self-respect. He believed that if a person didn't have these characteristics, then he wouldn't want them working at the factory.

As part of the hiring and continued working process, Ford's human resource department would conduct surprise visits to the workers' homes. If they lived in squalor or below the standard that was set by the company, the inspector would give them a warning. If the next time the inspector went to the home and found little or no improvement, that person would be fired.

On the surface, that may seem harsh, but also consider that Ford wanted to make sure that the people who worked for him lived a righteous life. If the worker was living with a significant other, Ford insisted that they would have to be legally married. If they weren't, they were given an opportunity to rectify it. If they didn't, they would be terminated from employment.

That need for a righteous life was not just steeped in moral considerations. It was also about efficacy. On the one hand, Ford held himself and those around him to high moral standards. Like Rockefeller, he was a teetotaler. He was also righteous in his dating life, having only dated Clara Jane Bryant, then marrying her, and staying married until the day he died.

Aside from his stringent moral sense and need for efficacy, Ford had a singular mind-set—to apply the requisite focus from everyone involved in the production of his cars. He wanted to boost efficacy and excellence in all things that he undertook. Ford was singularly focused on this goal.

Unlike his good friend Luther Burbank, the botanist, who was the total opposite of Henry in terms of spreading his focus across many different tasks, Henry would rise almost to the level of an obsession when he needed to solve a challenge.

That characteristic turned out to be the reason for his success, but it was also a stumbling block during the early part of his career. Even though he had a fairly easy beginning and a rather privileged youth compared with that of his neighbors, Henry kept floundering, allowing success to slip through his fingers because he demanded perfection from everything.

Perfection in daily life is elusive, and to demand perfection from pedestrian activities is a fool's errand, but Henry never understood that. It wasn't until he was neck-deep in designing the assembly process that his strict codes of conduct surfaced and paid off.

This same mentality caused him to reject formal schooling. Being in school seemed to be a waste of time for him—not because he would rather be out playing—but more because he would rather be investigating or learning something more substantive.

What was Henry's problem?

Aside from his meticulous and almost obsessive behavior, he was a perfectionist. That was one problem. On the other hand, he wanted to accomplish so much. Even at a young age, he wanted to get involved in so many things (all related to mechanization) and also wanted to dig deep into everything.

You may be a jack of all trades but a master of none. It is not really possible to be the master of all trades. Yet, that is exactly what Ford aspired to be. That dichotomy created immense demons within him.

Not only did he want to solve problems that existed, but he also wanted to find solutions for problems that most people did not even know existed. Imagine what it must have felt like to see a challenge and then try to find solutions that didn't exist.

It's similar to when one realizes the number of pesticides that are being used in the production of food and know this is a big problem. With this problem, they go about finding a solution, which is to switch to organic foods. Problem solved . . . and they move on. But what if there was no solution? What if there was no organic food? How do you match a solution to a problem when there is no existing solution? How many people would go about structuring the solution to that problem? Yet, that is exactly what Ford did with the automobile industry. He may have started out with a simple goal of making affordable cars, but what he wound up doing was creating a method of production that squeezed every ounce of efficiency from materials, labor, process, and design. It was revolutionary.

To be clear, Ford's life was not just about cars. He had a family that stood behind him, and he had concerns just as any father and husband have. He also had personal concerns and weaknesses that plagued him. His only confidante on these matters was Clara. She knew him best.

Even though he was a genius on the outside, he could not decipher and detect the problems inside him. He could not solve the demons within him. He was too much of a perfectionist that it troubled him to let go of something that was not yet perfected. It was this characteristic that led him to designing and building the River Rouge plant. One could not do something so detailed and exacting without being obsessive in nature.

That obsession allowed him to dig deeper at every stage of the inquiry be it design or his vision—whether it was taking apart the pocket watch his father presented him when he was twelve or building a better four-stroke engine and understanding the problem of gasoline and air mixture. Once he put his mind to it, he couldn't and wouldn't let go until it was resolved.

We all agree that Ford was smart, but most people seem to miss that his intelligence was not just some abstract and ephemeral quality that existed in the recesses of his brain. It was a practical and well thought out plan that he could visualize. He could hold detailed images of what he wanted in his mind while he built the steps needed to get to what he could visualize.

Take, for instance, the pocket watch his father gave him when he was twelve. Most people at that age have a hard enough time focusing on reading a chapter in a book. Ford, however, was able to observe the mechanisms in the watch and not only remember the parts but also where they went. More importantly, Ford could see which came first and which came later. That is three-dimensional thinking. It was the same skill he

↑ Ford invents the carburetor.

used when he built the River Rouge plant thirty years later.

It was this intense cerebral process and observation ability that resulted in his designing and patenting the first carburetor. It was this invention that increased the power output of the internal combustion engine. Today, it is not easily found in automobile engines since it has been replaced by electronic fuel injection. In Ford's time, however, it was a revolutionary addition to the engine.

Even though he designed his cars and thought of good innovative ideas for the improvement of the car, the invention of the car itself is not his to claim. Not even the invention of the carburetor could suggest that he had anything to do with the car or the engine that Karl Benz or Gottlieb Daimler had invented.

We hear more about Ford than Benz and Daimler because Ford had a larger impact on the automotive world, the social structure of the last generation, and the well-being of the generations that followed. And that was just the knock-on effect that came from production of his

Ford's assembly line is used in manufacturing everything from iphones to tractors.

inexpensive cars. But there is more. Ford's assembly line is now used in manufacturing everything from iPhones to tractors.

In fact, the entire academic world is designed based on the needs of the modern manufacturing system. There is a pyramid-shaped organizational chart that has the largest number of workers on the factory floor who are controlled by a smaller number of supervisors, who are controlled by an even smaller number of managers and so on as it goes all the way up to the CEO of the company. In the same way, high schools and technical institutes pump out more graduates than colleges that pump out more graduates than regular graduate schools and they, in turn, pump out more than Ivy League business schools. Those two pyramids intersect.

Harvard Business School (and the other top business schools) grads are the most likely to sit on top of that pyramid, which was created by Henry Ford when he perfected the manufacturing system. A country's success is determined by how well those pyramids are shaped.

That is how deep Henry Ford's influence has extended to society today. It was all based on the manufacturing assembly line model.

The problem he focused on and solved was more than just industrial engineering. It was also in economics. The improvements in such factors as the assembly line, human resources, Just in Time inventory management, and cost management were all part of what came out of Ford's endeavor to create the most cost-effective product.

He realized what the top business schools teach today as part their curriculum. He realized that a product seen from the customer's perspective is different from a product as seen from the manufacturer's point of view.

The customer sees a product as a solution to a problem. The manufacturer, while cognizant of the problem and the method to solve that problem, sees the solution (the product) as an integrated string of tangible and intangible steps. Ford saw the solution to mass independent mobility as a catch-22. He clearly saw when no one else did that to produce at such a low process they need to sell a large volume. To be successful, they needed large facilities that were fully integrated. It was all connected like the gears in the pocket watch his father had given him all those years ago.

Ford is remembered today because he solved that equation. He did all this without any tertiary education during the interregnum period straddling the two industrial revolutions.

The Industrial Revolution that preceded the mid-nineteenth century set up the environment in which the North was able to mechanize more than the South. It was all built on Ford's plant design and philosophy. His method created better efficiency for industry.

The First Industrial Revolution also affected social structure. There was a move from cottage industries to factories, which resulted in rural/urban migration. It was the start of the move toward the building of large cities.

Before Ford's arrival on the scene, the entire world was primarily agrarian. It wasn't much different from John Ford's farm in Ireland.

Everyone worked the farm with their hands, hand tools, and beasts of burden.

The social dispersion of societies was flung far and wide over farms. It's much like driving through the rural farms of Maine or the ranches in Nevada. They were dispersed.

Then came the First Industrial Revolution that changed society. Since factories that were powered by steam and coal were centralized, the working population had to live in the cities for work. Cities back then were dirty and smoggy. So came the first urban migration.

Then came a gap in the revolution of industry. The mid-nineteenth century saw a brief respite in innovation, but the next revolution saw even more innovation. This is where Henry Ford's contribution is important.

The First Industrial Revolution had solved issues in two areas: (1) infrastructure expansion, with iron and coal being the core of mechanization and power and (2) solving individual and specific problems. Steam was the new energy resource, and to make steam, one needed coal to fire up the water.

As for the second aspect of the First Industrial Revolution, they were innovations in mechanization. Take, for instance, the spinning jenny. It was a multispindle spinning machine that increased the speed of the job that would be done by one person. That meant that one machine didn't replace one person. It increased the output of that person. That increased output would translate to better dispersion of overhead costs and better consumer adoption.

The Second Industrial Revolution was a totally different set of innovations. It also had two aspects to it; for the first, think of such men as Rockefeller in oil, Carnegie in steel, and Edison in electricity. Their innovations completely altered the landscape of business and opportunity. It was now the Gilded Age and unprecedented prosperity in America.

The Second Industrial Revolution straddled the use of softer factors, and while it did have some forms of increased mechanizations the Second Industrial Revolution. Not only were machines, factories, and contraptions making mass production easier, but new innovations were also coming online faster than at any time in the past. With the U.S. patent law taking effect in 1790, innovators and inventors had come out in full force.

People like Edison set up offices and businesses to innovate and commercialize products. The United States and to a large extent the rest of the industrial world had created machines to take on industries of the past, but other industries were to come.

Take car manufacturing, for instance, which was something that would evolve in the next half-century and not be geared toward being produced by other machines. This was the basis of the Second Industrial Revolution.

Henry Ford's good fortune as a young child gave him the time and ease to think about things that were not always a pressing matter for most other people. He had loving parents and a father who was not prone to any of the bad habits that many were at the time.

By the time he was born, the hard living conditions that the Fords before him had faced were in the past. Henry's father was well to do and respected. Whatever hardships that Henry Ford would come to know about would be from the stories his father told him through the years.

Those stories did not remain distant imagery and fodder for a rainy afternoon. They seemed to have stuck in his mind with intensity that is usually not characteristic of a child. As he grew older, the stories became more serious, and he later learned that his paternal grandmother had passed away on board a ship. It was the first instance for him coming face to face with death and the loss of a loved one.

Henry also had a deep sense of belonging. He took his name seriously and knew that it was his name that bestowed value to the life he would contribute to those around him.

The shift from a wartime economy to a postwar economy also had a significant effect on Americans. Industrialization had increased, and mechanization was beginning to form the basis of higher technologies. In Pennsylvania,

Carnegie was developing better ways to make steel. In Ohio, Rockefeller was bringing refineries and technology online, and in New York, J.P. Morgan was revolutionizing the financial world.

No doubt there was a generational gap between Carnegie, Morgan, Rockefeller, and Henry Ford, but all these served as the foundation for the Second Industrial Revolution.

Henry Ford's development of the Model T and the subsequent rise in the number of households that owned vehicles was significant in how John D. Rockefeller increased his wealth. Wealth may have been a driving factor for Rockefeller, but it was never just about the wealth when it came to Ford. In fact, just before he was able to get the idea for his vehicle produced, he was down and out on his luck.

Ford had taken loans and investments that were not yet panning out, which was stressful. It was Clara who held it together for him and got him to focus on what he needed to do.

Family

Clara had always been the force that held the family together for Henry. He was used to having a strong family support structure, even if he did lose his mother early in life. He had his siblings, his grandparents, and his father not to mention a whole host of cousins and their respective families.

When he was growing up, he had close relationships with his immediate family. He was set in his ways and not comfortable around strangers. Henry grew up in a full house. His father showered him with attention, and his mother was immensely close to him and taught him to read and did a good job of homeschooling him long before he went to a private school. His maternal grandfather would also take him around the farm and introduced him to the animals that roamed around and showed him flowers.

Between his mother and his maternal grandmother, he had a solid introduction to the power of nature and the beauty of farming. His father, uncles, and grandfathers were his role models and had a solid history of farming, and his introduction to nature was not just about the technical aspects of the earth but also about the almost spiritual aspects of being one with the creation and regenerative forces of the land.

This spiritual background and the fact that William was a deacon gave Henry a solid foundation in life. Although he would later not have much interest in organized religion and instead embraced more Eastern philosophies, the core of his spirit was always about doing the right thing. He was more about the spirit than about the commandment, more about being righteous than about being rich, and certainly more about being a husband than about being a successful businessman.

Aside from his guidance on nature and spirituality, William expertly guided young Henry for a life on the farm by forcing him to work in different areas, which was something Henry deplored. It wasn't clear if his idea to mechanize farm operations was for the love of machinery or because he hated manual labor.

There was a sense of pride in the Ford and O'Hearn families of their heritage and farming in general. To be independent and respected, one had to put in the requisite toil and harvest the bounty of the earth, and the only way you could do that was by farming.

Henry, however, did not want to do that at all and actually disliked farmwork. He preferred dealing with machines but was not able to tend to his passion due to his duties on the farm. William was also a bit of a gearhead. Henry's eye on future technologies and mechanization was not developed in a void. It had a direct link and connection to the way William thought. Still, William did make Henry get his hands dirty and put him to work on the farm as soon as it was time to do so.

Ford enjoyed tinkering with machinery when he was young. His mother noticed this from a very young age said that he was "born a mechanic," as he wrote. His perspective, however, was that he wanted to find a better way to do farmwork, which made him enter the world of machines. Ford had a simple shed in which all his "tools" were kept, which were not really tools but just pieces of metal that he used as tools. Ford wrote in his autobiography, "In those days we did not have the toys of today; what we had were home-made. My toys were all tools—they still are! And every fragment of machinery was a treasure."

This writing shows how much he absolutely loved machinery. For most children, marbles and wooden toys were their favorite things to play with. For Ford, he had fun tinkering.

When Ford was twelve years old, he used to see the steam-powered engine that would pass near his home while he and his family were going to the town. He would be so fascinated by it that when his father was driving the carriage, he would jump down to see the engine. He and the man who ran the engine would discuss the train, and the person who ran the train was more than happy to explain to young Ford how it and each part worked.

It was also during Ford's twelfth year that his father gave him a pocket watch. He very quickly became adept at dismantling and putting watches back together and soon became known as someone who could repair watches. Ford was in school until only his eighth year. Consequently, he did not know much about facts, dates, whos, whats, and wheres, but he did have a knack for knowing about machinery. He learned about machines by working with them and experimenting with them. His knowledge came from doing, not reading.

Ford wrote in his autobiography, *My Life and Work*, that one cannot really learn everything out of books. He said that one would learn better by doing—not just by researching. His opinion was that doing an action yielded more and was better than just reading. He was right. Doing is good; reading is good; both work even better.

From a very early age, Ford thought that farming could be improved. He would later succeed in building a lightweight tractor for farmers, making their jobs much easier. The cars he would later manufacture, such as the Model T, would also be of great help to farmers.

Ford's mother passed away in 1876. It was a hard blow for young Ford, and now there was no longer any reason for him to continue to stay at the farm. He would later write, "I never had any particular love for the farm—it was the mother on the farm I loved."

Chapter 4 Detroit

In 1879, Ford had just turned sixteen, and he wanted to advance his skills as a machinist and his knowledge of tools and metallurgy. He left the family farm in Dearborn and walked nine miles to the city of Detroit.

Once there he tried to get a job, but there weren't many for boys who grew up on the farm. He was specifically trying to find a job in factories or machine shops. If he were looking for a job as a factory assistant or something similar, it would not have been too much of a problem, but he was looking for a job that was typically done by a specialist. In today's terms, he was looking for an engineering job without an engineering degree.

Remember that Ford didn't have much formal education, and even though he was sharp, he had no paper qualifications. He spent some time looking for a job, but it wasn't easy. His father also tried on his behalf, contacting acquaintances in Detroit, but nothing seemed to work.

He finally found a job working for James Flower and Bros. Co. and later went on to have the same position at the Dry Dock Engine Works as a trainee. Ford would learn from this experience how to use engines. This knowledge later helped him develop engines for his Quadracycle. He found that making automobiles powered by steam engines would not work, as the power-to-weight ratio of the heavy steam engine would not be enough to adequately power a chassis loaded with goods and passengers.

Ford left Detroit in 1882 and returned to the Ford family farm in Dearborn. He worked on the farm for his father and adapted the farm engine made by the Westinghouse Company. He was so good that he taught the company representative how to work the machine better.

It was during Ford's time in Dearborn that he met his wife, Clara Jane Bryant. It was 1885, and they both attended a dance celebrating the New Year. He and Clara liked each other considerably from the very first time they saw each other.

Henry became distracted. It was the first time since he had turned sixteen that he had his thoughts on something other than his car or something mechanical.

For her part, Clara liked Ford for his knowledge of machinery as well as his tenacity and uncommon cerebral powers. Several years later and many years after their marriage when Ford was an influential figure in the United States, he said to the press, "The greatest day of my life was when I married Mrs. Ford."

The courtship between Ford and Clara was very wholesome indeed. They enjoyed boat rides, dancing, and corn husking. The two were engaged to marry by 1886, but Clara's mother thought that her daughter was still too young to get married and convinced them to wait until 1888. After all, she was three years younger than Ford and was only twenty years old by the time of her engagement.

Finally, on April 22, 1888, Clara's birthday, Henry Ford and Clara Jane Bryant became husband and wife. For the next five years, the couple tried for a child. Clara eventually became pregnant with Edsel Ford, their only son. Edsel was born in Detroit on November 6, 1893.

Ford loved his family deeply. He was very close to his wife, and when he was suffering from senility and partial dementia as well as several strokes in his later years, he would always want her in his sight, relying on her for safety, familiarity, and comfort. Initially, he was also very close to his son, but this seemed to change when Edsel grew up. Edsel's untimely death in 1943 was a stinging blow to Ford's emotional state and stability.

Chapter 5 The Ford Quadracycle

Over the next few years after the wedding, Ford would experiment and try to build a lightweight vehicle. After several years of experimentation, he built his first car in 1895. It was the Ford Quadracycle. He named it the "Quadracycle" because its *four* wheels were bicycle wheels. It was a simple car with a side plate at the front and a tiller to direct the car. There were just two speeds that the Quadracycle could travel at, and it was incapable of reversing. At the time, Ford's first car seemed like a bother. It held up traffic, frightened the horses, and was noisy.

Ford was about the only person driving a vehicle in Detroit at that time, and everyone was greatly interested in it, although it was a problem for the townsfolk. Ford said that when he was not by its side, people would come, get inside, and try to start it. They weren't doing it to steal the vehicle, but their curiosity pushed them to try to start it. Ford had to chain the vehicle to a lamppost whenever he stopped driving and left the car for a moment or two.

Ford drove his Quadracycle a thousand miles from 1895 to 1896 and then sold it to Charles Ainsley for $200. Ford was actually not planning to sell the Quadracycle in the beginning, but it turned out to be beneficial. Ford wanted to begin building a second car, and he needed funds for it.

When his new car was completed, it did not look any different from his first Quadracycle—but it did weigh less. At the time, Ford was using the belt drive in his cars, which worked well when the weather wasn't hot. It was this problem that later made Ford switch over and start using gears. When it was hot, the belts would expand and misalign with the drive and axle gears. This caused it to derail.

The year that Ford built his second Quadracycle a new model Benz automobile was on display in New York. Ford went to see it to get some ideas for his own invention, but he found nothing he could take from it and also found that it was considerably heavier than his own car. He wrote, "I was working for lightness; the foreign makers have never seemed to appreciate what lightweight means."

A couple of years after Ford sold his Quadracycle to Charles Ainsley, he bought it back for $100 from someone who had bought the car from Ainsley.

Ford liked machinery and gizmos so much that he had a room in his Dearborn house that was filled with what he called his "mechanical treasures." One of these was a dynamo that had been previously used at the Edison Illuminating Company.

He had some history with this particular dynamo. Ford had purchased the dynamo from another place that had purchased that dynamo from the Edison Illuminating Company. He had the dynamo upgraded and then installed it at the Canadian electrical plant that Edison's company was building. When the company was going to build another plant, Ford took the dynamo and placed it in his room of "mechanical treasures."

In the late 1890s, the Edison Illuminating Company, the company where he was working as Chief Engineer, offered him the position of General Superintendent, but it came with a condition. If Ford wanted to hold that position, he needed to drop all of his automotive activities and dedicate himself to the Edison Illuminating Company.

Ford was at a crossroads, the first of many in his life. He could choose to drop his vision and hold a prestigious position at one of the largest companies in the nation or he could risk it and strive to make his dream a reality.

Ford chose the latter. On August 15, 1899, he said goodbye to the Edison Illuminating Company and plunged headlong into the automotive business.

Quitting his job at the Edison Illuminating Company was risky. He did not have any money of his own. Despite the tight situation, however, Clara supported her husband in his decision.

How many of us today would do something like that?

It was during this time that Ford was part of the Detroit Automobile Company, founded in 1899. He was the engineer and in charge of the production of cars. The owners and other controllers of the company were not focused on making a car for the masses or creating a cheap, affordable car. They were more interested in creating expensive cars that the rich and wealthy could easily afford—they were focused on making money—that was their sole purpose. Ford, however, was not interested in that. He soon realized what the company was doing. He wrote, "And being without authority other than my engineering position gave me, I found that the new company was not a vehicle for realizing my ideas but merely a money-making concern— that did not make much money."

Ford spent his time experimenting and trying to make a car that would be affordable and available to the people. Meanwhile, the owners and investors of the company became upset, and to placate them, Ford assigned work to his thirteen workers to make parts for cars that he had no intention whatsoever of building.

Finally, when the investors felt that Ford was lagging too far behind, they dropped him, and Ford was left out in the cold. He resigned from the company on March 2, 1902. During his time with the company, it had been renamed the Henry Ford Motor Company, a purely honorary thing. After Ford left the company in 1902, the Lelands came to the company, and it became the Cadillac Motor Company.

Ford was then extremely upset with investors—he absolutely despised them. He never wanted to deal with them again, but he would in establishing the Ford Motor Company—but he would later force them out. After leaving the Henry Ford Motor Company, he rented a workplace at 81 Park Place and began experimenting.

At the time, people were interested in the automobile for racing purposes. They only cared to look at one that was fast. Ford was not building cars for that purpose, but he would soon have to change.

Chapter 6 ALAM & A Rising Star

On his own, to build his cars, Ford approached the Association of Licensed Automobile Manufacturers with his design of the car and was seeking their permission to manufacture and sell his cars. ALAM had the rights to the Selden Patent and the authority to say who sold cars and who didn't.

So, companies that wanted to make and sell their own cars needed to come to ALAM and ask for their permission. Ford was later rejected. He did not care, though, as he didn't need some monopoly's permission to do something. Despite ALAM's not allowing him to sell his cars, he went ahead and did it.

Before that, however, he needed to gain popularity to attract a market. So, he called for a race with Alexander Winton, who accepted the challenge, and the two raced at the track at Grosse Point in Detroit in October of 1901.

Ford built a special car for the race, the Ford Sweepstakes. It had a two-cylinder engine built very tight and rated high in compactness. Ford's Sweepstakes was incredibly fast, and it was then that he challenged Alexander Winton to a race.

Throughout the entire race, Ford was always lagging behind, and only on the sixth lap was he able to pass Winton, which happened because Winton's engine began to smoke, and it slowed Winton's vehicle, allowing Ford to pass. Ford's victory over the fastest race car driver in America made him a celebrity and famous. Everyone then knew his name—Henry Ford—the new fastest man in the United States.

Although Ford could not pass Winton for the first six laps, the fact that Winton's engine began to smoke and Ford's did not showed that Ford's car, a car that he built, was stronger and more durable that Winton's, proving that his car was better. Ford's victory gave him the idea of building a four-cylinder engine.

As people were only interested in a car that was fast, Ford had proved that his car was what they were looking for. People began to pay attention to him, and he was even able to attract some investors even though he didn't like them. Two notable investors were the Dodge brothers, John Francis and Horace. Then, in 1903, the Ford Motor Company was established.

During the first few months, they made the first Model A, which would be produced from 1903 until 1904. Thus, it was from here, that Ford's career began.

Chapter 7 The Ford Motor Company

After establishing the Ford Motor Company, Ford began selling his cars to the masses, and it did not go unnoticed by ALAM. The organization filed lawsuits against Ford for copyright infringement. The lawsuit was filed in 1903, but the case would only be heard in court in 1909.

Unfortunately, Judge Hough, the judge who was conducting the case, ruled against Ford on September 15, 1909. Ford's fellow automobile manufacturers—his competitors—took advantage of the defeat at once. The rumor had spread that if Ford had a lawsuit filed against him, then all those who owned a Ford car would be liable for damages.

Ford released an advertisement which said, "In conclusion we beg to state if there are any prospective automobile buyers who are at all intimidated by the claim made by our adversaries that we will give them, in addition to the protection of the Ford Motor Company with its some $6,000,000.00 of assets, an individual bond backed by a Company of more than $6,000,000.00 more of assets, so that each and every individual owner of a Ford car will be protected until at least $12,000,000.00 of assets have been wiped out by those who desire to control and monopolize this wonderful industry."

Ford had thought that potential customers of the Ford Motor Co. needed to be reassured, but he was mistaken. Potential customers and buyers were completely satisfied with purchasing from the Ford Motor Co., and the firm actually did better, selling eighteen thousand cars that year, which was more than they had sold the preceding year.

Ford said that the case against the ALAM monopoly was actually the best sort of advertising the company had received. People trusted and had confidence in the Ford Motor Co., and the affair led to the loss of power and authority that ALAM held. Ford wrote that he had complete confidence that they would come out victorious. That notion was justifiable—the Ford car was popular, cheap, and available for anyone who was earning money—everyone loved Ford and thus supported him.

As it turned out, ALAM did not really own the patent, and Ford won the case.

Henry was not someone who backed down from what he believed to be right, which is shown by this episode involving ALAM.

Chapter 8 Henry Ford and Thomas Alva Edison

A deep, penetrating history binds these two giants of history. Henry Ford used to work for Edison Illuminating Company, and he decided to work there because Edison, an avid inventor, was one of Ford's greatest heroes.

Edison, who was born in 1847, was sixteen years Ford's senior. He had invented the vote recorder in 1868. It was his first invention that was patented. Edison was twenty-two, and Ford was a toddler.

Since Ford was interested in all things new and all things mechanical, he avidly read innovative journals and articles, where he found a direct line of information to the world of gizmos and inventions. The one that struck him the most was Edison's. By the time he was reading all the journals, he was about nine years old and had seen the invention of the vote recording device that Edison had invented and patented.

Edison soon became Ford's hero, and Ford began to think in the same way as Edison. For Ford, Edison was larger than life. Ford also learned that Edison did not have any formal education and thought that formal education dulled the mind more than liberated it.

As Ford kept track of his idol's development, Edison kept churning out his inventions from his Menlo Park facility. There was still no electricity as yet, and the light bulb hadn't been invented. It was merely from Edison's lesser inventions (if one could label them as such) that Ford had already determined that Edison was brilliant.

Edison continued entertaining Ford's interest by coming out with the stock ticker the following year and other phonographic recording devices, all of which he patented.

By 1874, when Ford was just eleven, Edison had developed the quadruplex telegraph, which could transmit several messages simultaneously. It was patented and the rights sold to Western Union. Ford was watching intently. He was absolutely amazed that the patent was sold for $10,000. He did the math and realized that the amount of money his father had paid for forty acres of land ($600) was a fraction of the price of the rights of Edison's invention. This thrilled him—not because he saw the monetary value or gain—but he saw the price very differently from how most people did.

Ford had a particular view of money that he also shared with Edison. They didn't see money as a means to purchase happiness or fun; they saw monetary value as a valuation of their contribution. While both men were not interested in the commercial value of money (i.e., the ability to buy more things), what they were truly interested in was the validation they received from the valuation.

In this same vein, Ford watched carefully as Edison went from the sale of one patent to the next and was constantly producing inventions in his Menlo Park office.

Ford was also impressed by how Edison had gone about institutionalizing his invention process. Ford had seen how farming was done all around Dearborn, and it was a very tedious process of one person doing many tasks day in and day out. That was one of the things that he didn't like about farming. It was slow and mind-numbing, but many people were more than happy to do just one thing and do it repeatedly. He kept that at the back of his mind and would eventually use it in his assembly practice.

As for Ford, he watched how Edison created his inventions in an atmosphere where Edison would spark the idea, draughtsman would draw it up, machinists would make it, and then they would see how well it worked. Through the process of iteration, they would either make it work or abandon it because there was no way to make it cost effectively. He would shelve these ideas, knowing they would be able to make use of them sometime in the future.

By 1877, the phonograph had been invented, which was one of the inventions that made Edison famous. By this point, Ford was a busy teenager, and he was highly impressed with the phonograph, which he had not yet actually seen or experienced, but the descriptions of it were enough to peak his enthusiasm.

It would be sufficient to say that Ford was an ardent fan of Edison. Then came the invention that changed everything, including Ford's life and thought process. If the other inventions had been great, they were only the beginning, and nothing could really compare with the invention of the light bulb and the electricity generation and transmission that came about in 1880 (it was actually in 1879, but by the time Ford had heard about it was the next year).

He had read that Edison had taken an existing idea of a contraption that could illuminate an entire room without the need for kerosene, which is what they had been using at Greenfield. What was more interesting was that Edison had also invented the way to commercially make electricity in large quantities so that an entire township could be illuminated at the flick of a switch.

Ford was very impressed. Within two years, Edison had built the first commercial power generation plant in New York to supply homes in the city. That was the one that sent electricity to J.P. Morgan's house in New York—the first house to have power from the grid (Morgan had financed Edison).

This was a significant development in a number of ways. It taught Ford three things that influenced him in the future.

He realized that if you are going to do anything it has to be for the wider public, and it has to be in a way that changs their lives. Mechanization didn't just apply to factories but also to the general public. You see that today in a way that Ford saw it—you see it through YouTube in giving someone the ability to broadcast information. You also see it through the Web, and you are now even seeing satellite launches where there are nanosatellites that individuals can launch so that they have their own means of global communication. It all started with Edison, but it was Ford who institutionalized it.

Ford also learned that it was not so much the light bulb but the infrastructure behind it that made all the difference. It would not have been that important if Edison had gone ahead and perfected the light bulb and then just let it be. He had to create a robust infrastructure behind it, from the power generation plant to the copper wires that transmitted the power to the fuses, switches, and safety features that made it possible for the consumer to just flick a switch and have a bulb illuminate a room (without the smell of kerosene).

Edison also opened Ford's eyes, though he didn't very much like this part, to the inclusion of the moneyman in the equation. In Edison's case, he had used J.P. Morgan to finance some of his ideas. Morgan had seen the genius in Edison and realized that he could invest in Menlo Park and take a profit when products were commercialized.

Thus, Edison didn't need to worry about finances and was free to invent. Ford saw the genius in that, and he approached the Marburys when the time was right. The Marburys were the first to invest in Ford's ideas and were actually the ones who also financed the development of the carburetor. But the idea of bringing investors on board soon lost its appeal for Ford after he dealt with them firsthand.

These lessons were at the core of Ford's thinking. He realized that Edison was indeed a wizard and had a brilliant mind and kept close tabs on his progress.

By the time the Edison Illuminating Company came to Detroit, Ford was twenty-five years old and had been working in Detroit for almost ten years. He had left his family farm when he was sixteen and worked at various machine shops in Detroit. It was during this time that he became a certified machinist.

When there was a vacancy in Edison's company, he couldn't help himself and decided to seek employment from the company of his idol. Its director, James Hood Wright, interviewed him and offered Ford a job as an engineer. Clara, his new bride, supported him, as she did with everything Henry undertook in their long life together.

Within three years of getting the job, he had done so well and had proven himself to such a degree that he was promoted to Chief Engineer in 1893.

As Chief Engineer, his job was less hectic and less predictable. He was no longer working for a fixed number of hours during the day but instead was on call twenty-four hours a day. He was making more than $125 and had a comfortable life.

He would then stay at home and work on other things that interested him. If a problem arose, he would be dispatched to monitor, fix, or solve it. He would then promptly return home to wait for the next call.

This gave him a lot of time to pursue his own interests, which is when he started building the Quadracycle. In the meantime, many other branches of the Edison Illuminating Company were being established across the country. Each would have a different board of directors and different management policies. They all formed an association, and each year a convention would be held in New York. Edison always attended.

As Chief Engineer of one of the companies, Ford was given the opportunity to attend the 1896 convention held at the Oriental Hotel in Brooklyn, New York. As excited as he was, he remembered to take two things with him—a camera to capture his childhood idol and his Quadracycle.

At the meeting, he managed to capture a few photographs of Edison, which are now in the historical record, but more important was that he actually managed to meet Edison one evening at one of the banquets for the attendees. At this meeting, they had a short but pleasant conversation, and Ford was able to show Edison his Quadracycle.

That brief encounter did three things: (1) it served as the spark to a lifelong friendship, (2) it solidified his endeavor in automobiles, and (3) it made flesh what was once mythical. It was an absolutely joyous occasion for Ford.

Edison was impressed with Ford's creation. A number of other people at this time were also trying to make cars and commercialize them. It seemed that everyone was trying to build a car and make some money out of it. In fact, that was one of the reasons AMAL had stepped in to enforce their patents. They effectively blocked many people from trying to build cars.

Creating a car was an uphill battle. What went on in Ford's mind will always be unknown because he never discussed or wrote about it in his autobiography. What we have are his actions and concerns during each decision-making process as he developed a production model.

One thing, however, is clear: he was entering a field that was competitive, and he was not sure at each juncture which path to take. In fact, his efforts to build a viable and working model failed completely and spectacularly twice in his life, but the number of daunting decisions he had to make was significant.

That encounter with Edison made all the difference. Being impressed with the Quadracycle and that Ford had a patent on the carburetor, Edison told Ford that he should keep up with it. He said Ford needed to keep working at it, which was the only way to eliminate the bugs.

Edison also told him that he should make the car electric. He expounded on the benefits of electricity (pollution was not one of them), saying that it was the energy source of the future. Ford took him seriously and tried to make the car electric, and he even built an engine that would use electricity, but the technology of electrical batteries was not very advanced, and Ford was forced to choose the kerosene engine because that was what was available and needed to get the car to market as quickly as possible.

In fact, Ford even built an engine that worked on ethanol, but because of Prohibition and subsequent law ethanol was cost prohibitive as a possible fuel source.

After the convention, Ford returned to Detroit. He would later send letters and telegrams to convey wishes and update Edison on how his endeavors were going.

For his part, Edison was glad to make a friend in Ford and would write back to the young engineer as often as Ford would write to him. Their friendship grew over the years, and Edison had kept track of Ford's progress.

Their friendship by mail lasted sixteen years. While each man continued to develop his own life, they only kept in touch through telegrams and letters. When they finally met again, it was 1912, and they decided to take a vacation together.

Their destination was the Everglades, where they would be surrounded by nature. This was the first of more than fifteen trips the two men would take and be accompanied by others, including Harvey Firestone, the tire magnate; John Burroughs, the naturalist; and even President Harding.

The first trip involved Ford, Edison, and Burroughs. It was a classic trip, and they would ride in Ford automobiles on long-distance trips with Edison usually in the lead car and guiding the way.

They would spend the evening by a crackling fire while they discussed philosophy, Shakespeare, and Mozart. Burroughs would spice up the conversation with talks of nature and the bird calls he would teach Ford.

Edison would discuss advances in the science, and Ford would fix the cars when they broke down during any of the trips. One such trip saw the fan break off and rupture the radiator. By this point, Ford was already a well-known industrialist, and Edison was one of the most famous men in America. Still, it was Ford who got out, got his hands dirty, and fixed his car.

As the years rolled on, the annual trips, with various other luminaires, grew the number of Ford cars in the caravan that would drive off the beaten path. At its height, what started off as a quiet holiday for two men (or three) became a caravan of fifty cars. One was even outfitted with a portable refrigerator. The trips also started to include reporters and fully dressed waiters and chauffeurs.

After sixteen years, they slowed down and instead decided to just go somewhere on vacation. Ford decided to buy a house right next to Edison in Fort Myers. The two spent the winter months there with their families.

As Edison grew older and was eventually confined to a wheelchair, Ford bought one, too, and would accompany him, although Ford didn't need it. They would even race their wheelchairs and bump into each other for fun. They were as close as two friends could be. Their friendship was widely known, and even Edison's children and family knew how close they were.

When Edison passed, his eldest son found a test tube in his father's office. He thought of Ford and sealed the tube with paraffin wax and gave it to Ford. It was filled with air that Edison had breathed. It sits today in the Henry Ford museum.

Chapter 9 Ford and Edsel

Edsel Ford, the son of the great automobile manufacturer, was born November 6, 1893. He was the only child of Henry and Clara, and in his early life he made his father proud. From an early age, he began fiddling with cars and would follow his father to work and was generally enthusiastic about his father's business.

Edsel grew up to be a very nice and friendly person. Ford, however, was looking for his son to be a more serious, firm, and commanding figure. This was the main cause of Ford's later disappointment with his son.

Edsel was the kind of person who liked style and fashion. He partied with rich people, who Ford thought of as people who were good for nothing. Much to his father's dismay and anger, Edsel drank alcohol. Ford never drank liquor and did not allow it in his house. Ford wanted people he dealt with to have the same attitude, and he didn't want his son to drink alcohol. Edsel's habit drove Henry up the wall.

When Ford and his wife had built their home in Fair Lane, they constructed a bowling alley and a swimming pool inside the house. This was meant for Edsel, but, again, he was out having fun with other rich kids.

Henry Ford retired from Ford Motor Company in 1919 and made his twenty-five-year-old son president of the company. Ford wanted to kick investors out of the game. Two of them, the Dodge brothers, had caused some trouble for Ford, and he wanted them out.

Edsel's sudden rise to the presidency of the Ford Motor Company worried Ford's investors. The ploy was meant to scare them and make them want to back out of the company by selling their interests. Ford, now publicly out of the company, said that he was going to start another car manufacturing company and was going to hire several hundred thousand workers and sell cars for $300 or less. This price was less than the price of a Model T. This worried investors, and they soon sold their interests in the company, which was then in full control of the Ford family. Outside stockholders would only be a part of the Ford Motor Company after Edsel's son, Henry Ford II, took the president's chair following Henry Ford's death.

One great difference between Edsel and Ford was that Edsel was more about style, and Ford was more about practicality. The Ford Motor Company was producing Model T after Model T, with no change in system or appearance—which was what Ford liked. Edsel, however, wanted cars to look nicer. The automobiles manufactured by other companies were flashy and stylish—much to Edsel's taste.

Edsel always tried to convince his father to build a new model with a nicer appearance, but every time he proposed the idea his father always refused. It was only when Chevrolet began manufacturing stylish cars that were both good and functioned well that Ford would yield to building a new model. What happened was that the market by the late 1920s was not limited to buying just practical cars, such as the Model T. People now had enough money to buy more expensive cars that also looked better and were stylish.

Edsel pressured his father to make a new model, and Ford finally decided to do so. Edsel took charge of the chassis. He designed the body. If you pull up an image of the Model A, which was produced from 1927 or 1928 to 1931, it looked very stylish—much more than the Model T.

Unfortunately for Edsel, however, his father showered in the spotlight of the Model A, while he stood in the shadows watching his design be attributed to his father.

Over the years, great tension built up between Edsel and his father. Ford was upset that his son was mixing with the useless rich. He was upset that his son drank alcohol. He was disappointed with his son for his lack of firmness, authority, and fire. Instead, Edsel was a nice guy—not at all like the commanding figure Ford was.

Although Ford may have been hard and harsh on his son, he doted heavily on his grandchildren.

In fact, it may be said that Edsel's children got more pampering than Edsel did when he was a child.

Due to Edsel's activities, Ford had Bennett spy on him to keep tabs on what he was doing.

For a great part of Edsel's later life, his relationship with his father badly deteriorated, which perhaps made Edsel unhappy.

During the last few months that he was alive, Edsel had not been feeling right and was somewhat ill. In the end, it was found that he had end-stage stomach cancer. He underwent surgery as doctors tried to remove the tumor, but they were unsuccessful, and Edsel died prematurely. He had not told anyone of his condition, not even his father. The only person who knew about it except for his doctor(s) was his wife, Eleanor.

As Edsel lost more and more strength over time, Ford was upset, thinking that if his son stopped drinking so much and spent less time with those rich kids he would get better. Ford did not know what his son was going through.

Ford even sent someone to tell Edsel that he needed to fix a long list of things in his life, but upon hearing this, Edsel began to cry.

The stress Edsel was put under by his father was much too difficult for him to bear. One day, while at the office, Edsel fell to the ground. From that point on, he could not work and remained at home. When Eleanor told Henry what was actually going on and that Edsel was actually going to pass soon, Henry was in denial. Edsel passed away May 26, 1943, at only forty-nine years of age.

Edsel's death had a very devastating effect on Henry. The relationship between the two had been very uncomfortable for the last several years, and press videos in which they were both present showed the discomfort between them.

Edsel's untimely passing may have been the catalyst for Ford's senility. He died just four years later in 1947, and his last few years were not at all pretty. He became president of the Ford Motor Company once again but was not at all the same person he had been several years earlier when he handed over the company to his son.

After Ford died, the company produced a series of cars called the Edsel. They were supposed to be flashy and stylish, but they were not very popular and did not last long.

Chapter 10 The Mind of a Genius

Ford had only a few years of formal schooling and the apprenticeships in Detroit that enabled him to be certified as a machinist. That was the extent of his formal and semiformal learning. Everything else he learned on his own by the power and volition of his own intellect and vision.

We all have a certain level of genius within us. It is unfortunate that many still see the description of being a genius as an exclusive trait. It is seen as something that only a few people have, but that is not true. There is a genius in everyone.

In the words of Ford himself when he was designing the moving assembly line, he noted that most people were intelligent, but they chose to not be. He defined people in two categories: (1) those who were intelligent and smart and had the tenacity and mettle to do what was necessary and (2) those who were smart and intelligent but had no intention of putting in the work that was necessary. Henry labeled the former as a genius and the latter as lazy.

Ford did not care if a person was formally educated or went to school. He hadn't been and neither had his best friend, Edison. So when he interviewed factory workers who came to work for him, he would not ask for their qualifications or their certificates but would pose questions of intelligence to them where they would have to use their minds and think. There was not any real answer to the questions, but it would show a person's process of thinking.

In time, those who had no idea what the question meant were annoyed and wondered what the question had to do with turning a wrench, but that is the way Ford saw things. His intelligence was the same way.

Just like his father before him, Ford was a silent man in the presence of people other than his family. At work, he listened more than he spoke and thought more than he listened. Ford was the quintessential thinking man, which is what characterized his genius.

The problem with deep thinking is that it sometimes cuts out the forces of reality. It is sometimes hard to come out of one's own thoughts and apply them to the world outside. It is also hard for others around the thinker to realize what he is doing. Ford faced the same issue. For that, he had a solution: Clara.

Clara formed the bridge between him and the world around them. Without Clara, Ford would not be able to understand the world as he saw it and wouldn't be able to interpret his thoughts and apply them to the world around him.

Clare was also the bridge between Ford and Edsel. Ford wanted Edsel to have so much more than he did. He also wanted Edsel to advance the skill set and knowledge that Henry had fought to acquire. For this reason, he pushed Edsel in many ways. He loved Edsel but thought he was weak.

Because he knew he had to be tough to manage the Ford Motor Company, he wanted Edsel to be sharp and intelligent, which Edsel was but not in the way that Ford had envisioned. That was the core of the friction between the two men. Henry for his part, however, loved Edsel deeply. He just never got around to showing it in a way that Edsel understood.

The situation worsened after Ford hired Harry Bennett, a famous boxing champion and former Navy sailor, as head of security. Bennett was responsible for running a tight ship at the River Rouge plant. Ford become close to Bennett over the years and saw a strong man in charge of things who couldn't be pushed around. It was the same kind of perspective he had hoped for Edsel, but Edsel was nothing like that.

The closer Henry got to Bennett, the more he felt disappointed by Edsel's approach to things. Edsel was more refined and thoughtful. Bennett was rough and direct. Bennett was the embodiment of what Henry wanted Edsel to be.

Because of this gap, it fell on Clara to be the bridge yet again between Henry and their son. Whether this helped or was more detrimental is hard to determine, but Clara always tried to bring the two men together.

The mind of a genius, especially in Ford's life, was both a boon and a curse. He could decipher the problem that others didn't even know existed and then fashion a solution to it inside his head. What didn't come to him naturally was the business aspect of it. That was just in the beginning. As time passed, he grew more adept with management style, and his ability to foresee the business angle of things allowed him to be one step ahead of the game.

Ford had ideas far beyond what most men could see—even his investors. The investors who financed Ford in his business were not willing to spend as much as he wanted, which led to friction on both sides.

When Ford first brought on investors, he didn't know how the investment and private equity world functioned. Financiers ended up dictating what Ford could and could not do, and he soon realized that his vision differed greatly from theirs. They were all about the bottom line with a short-term horizon; he was all about customer growth and satisfaction and a long-term horizon.

These were basic differences. When they first got together, no one really understood or appreciated how shrewd Ford really was. Once he had learned how the financing world worked, he did not like the way he was being pinned down to do things he didn't like, so he played a ruse on them.

He started off by making Edsel chairman of the company. That alone caused everyone to feel a little uncomfortable. Then he told them that he was getting ready to start his own car production company, which caused all his investors to find a buyer for their stock, and Ford scooped them up at a low price.

The genius of Henry Ford is evidenced in two ways. For a boy from the farmlands of Michigan who never had formal schooling, he certainly understood how high corporate finance worked.

He also knew human nature very well and knew what the investors would do when he behaved a certain way. In this instance, he and Rockefeller had the same way of thinking.

To draw a comparison between Rockefeller and Ford, just consider a similar episode that took place in Rockefeller's business life.

In January 1865, when oil was struck in Pithole, Rockefeller asked Clark to sign for another loan. Clark was incensed and didn't keep quiet. He said to Rockefeller, "We have been asking too many loans in order to extend this oil business." Rockefeller replied by saying, "We should borrow whenever we can safely extend the business by doing so."

To check Rockefeller, the three Clark brothers tried to intimidate him by saying they would break up the relationship between the partners by ending it. To do this, all partners needed to agree, which would mean the end of the business. This was not the first time or the last that they tried to intimidate him by threatening dissolution, but Rockefeller had wised up to the trick and decided to use it to his benefit.

Rockefeller wanted to end his relationship with the Clark brothers and was finished with working in his current business of selling and buying on behalf of others. Rockefeller was successful in getting Andrews to join him in his venture and break off from the Clark brothers.

He said to Andrews, "Sam, we are prospering. We have a future before us, a big future. But I don't like Jim Clark and his habits. He is an immoral man in more ways than one. He gambles in oil. I don't want this business to be associated with a gambler. Suppose I take them up the next time they threaten a dissolution. Suppose I succeed in buying them out. Will you come in with me?"

Andrews agreed to join Rockefeller since he, too, could plainly see that his fortunes would fare better by staying with Rockefeller than the crazy Clark brothers. Several weeks later the trigger for Rockefeller to enact his plan took place. He had an argument with his first Clark partner, who said he would break up the partnership of the produce firm. "If that's the way you want to do business we'd better dissolve, and let you run your own affairs to suit yourself."

On February 1, 1865, Rockefeller prepared for the final blow. He called his partners to his home and talked about how they could expand their business in a way he knew the Clark brothers would absolutely dislike. Jim Clark tried to intimidate Rockefeller into backing off by saying, as before, "We'd better split up." Rockefeller then asked everyone to say whether or not they supported the breaking up of the partnership. They all did, but they were merely using it to threaten him and when they left his house that night, they thought nothing of it and were confident they had gotten the better of him.

After the Clarks left his home, Rockefeller quickly rushed over to the *Cleveland Leader* newspaper office and demanded that an announcement be printed in the papers that the partnership was breaking up. The newspaper ran the notice in the next morning's edition, and before even getting to the office, the brothers saw it.

When the Clark brothers saw this announcement, they were stunned. Rockefeller's first partner, Maurice B. Clark, asked Rockefeller, "Do you really mean it? You really want to break it up?" Rockefeller replied by saying, "I really want to break it up."

In the end, it was decided that the oil refinery division of Clark and Rockefeller would be auctioned off. It turned out that the bidders for the auction were Clark and Rockefeller themselves. Essentially, the buyout would mean that the company would go to either the Clark brothers or Rockefeller.

By this point, Rockefeller was a man who could handle the most difficult situations with ease. His character was also such that when the people around him became more upset he became even more poised.

When the Clark brothers went to the auction, they had a lawyer with them who was the auctioneer himself. Rockefeller, however, did not bring a lawyer of his own. He thought he could handle it himself.

The bidding began at $500. It then increased to several thousand dollars. Then it reached $50,000, $60,000, and $70,000. By this point, Rockefeller was afraid that he would not be able to make the purchase. Then, the Clarks put up $72,000. Rockefeller quickly bid $72,500. Clark let go at that point, and Rockefeller asked, "Shall I give you a check for it now?" Clark denied it and said Rockefeller could pay when he was ready. It was a gentlemanly gesture, and he was shocked that Rockefeller had amassed that much money to make the purchase.

It turned out that Rockefeller's strategy of being prudent and being bankable worked to his favor. When the time came, he had lined up a line of credit from the banks that supported his takeover of the company. It was with their backing that he had the strength and tenacity to bid the price up to that level.

The price of $72,500 in 1865 would be about $1.2 million today. Although the price was high for the time, it was an important purchase. Rockefeller was just twenty-five years old and owner of the largest oil refinery in Cleveland, which was refining five hundred barrels of oil every day. Approximately two weeks after the Clarks met with Rockefeller in his home, the *Cleveland Leader* announced that Rockefeller had purchased the firm of Andrews, Clark, and Company. It went on to say that Rockefeller had purchased all the materials of the company, and that work would continue under the firm of Rockefeller and Andrews.

Both Rockefeller and Ford had learned how to take on those who had leverage over them. They managed to get out of the binding agreement in a way that was smart and clean. In Rockefeller's case, it was the Clark brothers; in Ford's, it was the Dodge brothers.

In the case of Henry Ford, there was a significant difference in doing business that is not widely practiced today. Both despised unions. Although in Rockefeller's time there were no unions, there was the burgeoning pressure on trusts, and the government was interested in breaking up trusts. In Ford's time, the government was trying to instill labor laws, and with that came labor unions.

Ford did not believe in labor unions any more than Rockefeller believed in antitrust laws. Both of them stood fast against the government overreach. Ford, being the genius that he was, saw how the people in his factories needed to do their work. He was not interested in keeping them as slaves, but he was strict that their hands were his when they were on the clock.

Bennett helped him in this regard. Bennett hired thugs and gangsters whom no one else would employ because of their criminal record. Bennett would make the rounds around the River Rouge plant, and he would not allow people to take breaks or chit-chat during working hours.

Ford treated his workers with respect and paid them well. He did not discriminate in hiring policies. He would just as soon hire nonwhites as whites, and he would just as soon hire those with physical disabilities as someone in perfect health. His concern was whether or not the person had the intelligence to work and the honesty to put in a good day's worth of work.

In this way, he did not encourage extended breaks and chatter during the assembly line process. How could he? The profitability of the company was based on how many cars could come off the assembly line. At one point, the Ford Motor Company was producing over a thousand cars per day.

Most people were in awe with the number of cars that were produced in a fully integrated plant such as the one in River Rouge, but they failed to see that to be successful Henry had to be strict with the policies of how the workers did their job. If they were busy chatting and not doing the work, one of two things would happen: (1) the line would slow down, which would result in fewer cars per day and increase the cost per unit or (2) the quality of the assembly, whether they were making finished cars or assembling magnetos, the quality of the product would suffer if employees were distracted by chatter. This is why Ford was strict about talking on the job.

Unions had a problem with this policy. Unions wanted the workers to be given the freedom to do certain things, and the collective bargaining they had was a disruption to work in Ford's eyes.

In that way, Ford and Carnegie were not different.

Carnegie had quelled a strike, popularly known as the Homestead Strike. During that time, Carnegie's head of security brought in mercenaries, or paid security professionals, to break up the strike. It was no different from what Ford did decades later at his plant.

At the River Rouge plant, Bennett's goons had beaten men who were urging the workers to unionize. The men were beaten up badly and then forced out of the factory. In the end, they managed to prevent the start of a union at the plant. That didn't last long, however, and Clara later convinced Ford to let the unions come into the factories.

The mind of a genius sees things in only one way—in this case, Ford wanted to put a car in every garage, and to do that he had to make it affordable. To make each unit affordable, he had to push the assembly through the plant at the best rate possible. He couldn't achieve the best rates when the men were chatting and taking time off.

That was why he was paying above-market rates, which provided two benefits: (1) it gave him a steady stream of workers so that he could boot out anyone who was not working well without worrying if he could replace that man and (2) he could tell them to do what he wanted without cause for revolt. But the unions would alter that equation. Even though he paid them well, the unions would ask for things that would slow down the production levels of the assembly line.

What he didn't see, however, which is what others saw, was that to the outside it looked as though he was driving a slave factory. How else would it look when you had guards walking around the plant and beating up anyone who was not working and then not allowing them to unionize?

Conclusion

Different men need to be looked at differently if you want to understand them on a deeper level. As much as we all share common traits, each of us is made unique by virtue of our experiences, our environment, our heritage, and our perception. We are further made different by the times we live in and our friends.

In the case of Henry Ford, many things affected him. Most important were his parents. He was extremely close to his father, but he was significantly closer to his mother. Her sudden passing was a blow that turned him inward. That event drew him closer to his father. The loss of his mother at a young age drew parallels in his mind between the circumstances he experienced and those his father had endured on board the Coffin Ship.

Besides his parents, Henry Ford was significantly influenced by Thomas Edison. The first layer of that influence came from his admiration as a young boy. The next layer resulted from the talks and correspondence he had with Edison. It was something that shaped his mind and moved his heart.

The challenges he faced in building his car and dealing with the patent infringement lawsuit with ALAM would have been enough to cause any man to give up and move on, especially since he was easily employable after his stint at Edison Illuminating Company. But it was Edison's words when they first met to "keep at it," referring to the Quadracycle, that made him relentless in his pursuit of the automobile.

For Ford, his relationship with his son was his greatest disappointment—not that Edsel was bad or behind at anything. Edsel was compassionate and smart in his own right. He had the pulse of the new generation, and his contributions were significant for the company's prosperity, but Henry's disappointment was about the way he treated his son. Henry, to the pain of any father, outlived his son, which gave Henry plenty of time to ponder and regret his actions.

To be clear, Henry did not neglect his son or love him any less. In fact, Edsel was the light of his life, and when he built the house in New York, he had specifically built up the grounds and included a tennis court so that Edsel could play his favorite sport. Henry wanted to raise a son who was independent and sharp—the way Henry was. What Henry missed was that Edsel had strengths in other areas. During the course of trying to raise his son in a way that Henry saw fit, he crossed his son in many ways that made Edsel feel unwanted and incompetent. But Henry had no such judgment against his son. Nonetheless, Edsel felt heartache before he died, and his father was heartbroken after Edsel died.

The sharpest pain for Henry came after Edsel died from cancer, and he started to realize the differences they had and was told by a close confidant that Edsel faced many difficult moments under his father. To this revelation, Henry asked this confidant if he had been cruel to Edsel. The man said he hadn't been cruel but was unfair.

That stayed with Henry for a long time and was something that he could never forgive himself for or forget.

The greatest influence in his life and the star that shone brightly for him was his wife. Clara was there through all the toils and challenges a young man could ever face all the way to the point when Henry lost control of his mind. The several strokes and the pain of losing his son had stretched his mind to the point of fracture, and it was Clara who held it together for him in the end—the same way she had always held him together and encouraged him.

The end was no different from the beginning. He and Clara were so in love with each other and had become so much a part of each other that even when Henry Ford had lost his mind he could not forget her.

During the last eleven years of his life, Ford suffered strokes. The first occurred in 1938, which was after the River Rouge plant had been completed. Production and operations were running fast, and the company had grown to a size that he was not sure Edsel could handle, but even though he was significantly slower than before, he continued. By this point, Edsel was also not in the best of health, but he still showed up for work every day, something that Henry did not fully understand. From that point, Henry had several other strokes, and each stroke left him weaker than the one before.

The strokes started to increase in frequency, and he was in precarious health after the passing of Edsel Ford in 1943. By this point, Bennett had taken charge of much of the operations, and Ford trusted him. Clara, on the other hand, didn't and thought Henry was being unkind to Edsel. She did not like the way Henry treated Bennett any better than Edsel, and she made it known as strongly as she could. However, it was hard to argue with Henry while he was stubborn and not always lucid after the first stroke.

After Edsel's passing, Clara eased up and decided to just focus on Henry. She was still strong and robust compared with him. By April

1947, Henry was weak and relied on Clara more than ever before. Not only was his body frail and he was unable to walk long distances or sit up straight for very long, but his mind was also not always clear, lucid, and coherent. He would often ramble in conversation.

It reached the point that he would follow Clara everywhere, and he was never fully aware of his surroundings. His last stroke took every last measure of his cognitive and physical ability. He was placed on his bed, and Clara had the housemaid call the doctors who were a few hours away. The conversation he was having before he died was about Edsel. After the stroke and while he was in bed, he didn't say anything. It was most likely that he had finally lost all ability to converse. He was restless, and Clara propped him up with more pillows. He recognized her, though, and sought refuge and safety in her arms. That seemed to comfort him, and he was at ease for the moment.

After some time had passed, he wanted the lights extinguished in the room, as they bothered him. The maid turned the lights out and opened the door so that the light from the other room would provide some illumination to an otherwise pitch-dark room.

As he sat up, more pillows were added for his comfort, but instead he chose to lean and rest his head on Clara's chest. The two of them had been inseparable for almost sixty years since they married. It was April 7, 1947, just four days short of their fifty-ninth wedding anniversary.

As his breathing began to struggle once again, Clara soothed him by stroking his hands and patting his forehead, all while wondering how long it would take for the doctor to arrive.

As she kept him company and whispered in his ear, Henry became more peaceful. His breathing stabilized, and he appeared to be at peace. Being on Clara's chest was the only place he wanted to be.

By 11:30 that night, all had fallen silent, and Clara realized that the doctors wouldn't be there anytime soon and this was going to be the end. She remained strong for her Henry just as she had been through all his struggles and through all his medical conditions, and she had even been there for him while he grieved deeply for the loss of his only son.

As she sat beside him holding the frail body of the giant of the automobile industry, she could feel the changes in his breathing until it finally stopped. She held onto him for a little while longer and then gently placed him on his back. The genius who was responsible for mass production of the automobile and personal freedom, the man who pioneered and perfected inventory management and assembly line effectiveness died at 11:40 p.m. on April 7, 1948. He had lived a full life, a fullness defined by the contributions he had made.

The *San Francisco Chronicle* wrote that "Henry Ford was comparable only to Christopher Columbus in his impact on civilization in the west."

No truer words have ever been spoken.

If you enjoyed learning about Henry Ford, I would be forever grateful if you could leave a review. Reviews are the best way to help new authors get feedback and also help your fellow readers find the good books. Thanks in advance!

Made in the USA
San Bernardino, CA
22 July 2020